{ CITIESCAPE }

TOKYO *

{ CITIESCAPE }

ANDREW BENDER

CONTENTS *

VITAL STATS *

{ }

NAME Tokyo **AKA** Eastern Capital
DATE OF BIRTH circa 1600 when Edo became
Japan's political capital. In 1868 the emperor
moved here and Edo was renamed Tokyo.
HEIGHT 6m **SIZE** 2187 sq km
ADDRESS Japan **POPULATION** 12.3 million

PEOPLE *

{ *TOKYO IS THE WORLD'S LARGEST METROPOLITAN AREA – OVER 25% OF THE }
JAPANESE POPULATION LIVES HERE, or 5900 people per square kilometre. But it's
no melting pot. The permanent population is overwhelmingly Japanese. Japanese is
the only universally spoken language; most Tokyoites have studied English, but few feel
comfortable speaking it.

IN A 2LDK apartment (two bedrooms with a living, dining and kitchen area), perhaps
a 12-minute walk from a subway station, might live a husband (salaryman), his wife
(stay-at-home mother) and their one adult daughter (Tokyo's birth rate is below 1%).
Young Tokyoites have for generations lived with their parents until marriage, often to
help with the care of a grandparent. This young woman has a job that pays well enough
for her to live on her own; she may pay rent, but she likely spends her disposable
income on designer shoes and European vacations instead.

9.

ANATOMY *

{ ***TOKYO'S FULCRUM IS THE IMPERIAL PALACE, BUILT ON THE SITE OF THE EDO CASTLE OF THE TOKUGAWA SHŌGUNATE,** and now the seat of the imperial family. To its east lie the financial districts of Marunouchi and Nihombashi and the grand department stores of Ginza, with the Sumida River to the east emptying into Tokyo Bay and the Pacific. Northeast of the palace are hilly Ueno Park and the old shitamachi (low city) of Asakusa. West of the palace are the national government buildings in Akasaka, the nightlife districts of Roppongi and Shibuya, trendy Aoyama and Omote-sandō, and the neon canyons of Shinjuku. }

DUE TO DISASTERS and demolitions, few pre-20th-century buildings remain. In their place is a fascinating mix of *Blade Runner*–style high-rises, some of the world's most forward-looking contemporary architecture and graceful parks and religious sites.

THE ENTIRE CITY is connected via a rāmen-bowl network of subways, trains and private rail lines. One point of reference for Tokyoites is the Yamanote Line, which loops around the city centre.

PERSONALITY *

{ ***UNIFORM, MONOLITHIC, BUSY, OVERPOWERING. THAT'S TOKYO AT FIRST GLANCE.** But scratch (just) below the surface and you'll find that the Japanese capital is a jumble of contrasts, thoroughly engrossing and demanding to be seen. }

WHITE-GLOVED LADIES in fine European ensembles, carrying ¥100,000 handbags in the crooks of their arms brush elbows with girls in Goth make-up and satin punk dresses; and when they do, they'll each bow, cover their mouths and utter a demure 'Sumimasen' (Excuse me). A sushi chef makes nigiri as Ella Fitzgerald plays in the background. The blue-suited salaryman on the subway opens his briefcase to reveal a stack of manga (comic books). A centuries-old samurai garden with a teahouse on a pond is overlooked by a forest of office towers, which in turn house tatami rooms where the samurai of that garden would feel right at home.

AS THE POLITICAL, financial, commercial, fashion, technology, media and cultural capital of the world's second-largest economy, Tokyo crackles with energy yet is never too busy for tea. It may export earth's latest and greatest, yet business relationships go back decades, even generations.

13.

TOKYO TRACES ITS history back to the early 1600s, when the shōgun (military leader) Tokugawa Ieyasu made a swampy, backwater town called Edo his capital. The seat of the imperial family remained in Kyoto, several hundred kilometres to the west; the arrangement served both cities well. While Kyoto turned its attention to the classical, Edo busied itself with the official and the profitable.

A MASSIVE BUREAUCRACY of feudal lords, attended by their families and protector samurai warriors, lived in central Edo's yamanote (high city); commoners from the hinterlands flooded into the outer shitamachi (low city). Dress, living quarters and speech were strictly codified, and interclass movement prohibited. Yet the Edo Period also saw one of the greatest flourishings of art and culture the world has ever known: woodblock printing and kabuki theatre, books and boats, tea ceremony and poetry.

TWO-AND-A-HALF centuries later, this elaborate feudal structure collapsed under its own weight, and in 1868 Emperor Meiji consolidated the political and imperial capitals in Edo, renaming the city Tokyo (Eastern Capital). Another boom ensued, during which train lines were built and Western-style architecture, dress, art and cuisine appeared – a massive earthquake in 1923, followed by World War II bombs, virtually levelled the city. The post-war period brought reconstruction, reconstitution and commerce. Exports of cars and electronics fuelled an overseas buying binge in the 1980s, followed by a trenchant recession in the 1990s from which Tokyo has finally and gratefully emerged.

TODAY'S TOKYO IS Hello Kitty and Ultraman, worldly and homebound, brazen and reticent, gracious and unremitting, unravelled and buttoned-up, exotic and safe – the chapters following offer a few glimpses. This city has seen its ups and downs – political turmoil, destruction, Godzilla – but Edokko (as the children of Edo are called) weather it all with grace, humility, optimism and perhaps Tokyo's most defining feature: style.

14.

GRACIOUS*

{ *VIEW IT FROM A TOWER OBSERVATORY, SPEND AN HOUR ON A TRAIN, OR JUST CROSS THE STREET, AND IT'S INSTANTLY OBVIOUS. Tokyo is massive, the world's largest metropolitan area. Yet the visitor expecting the usual big-city ills – squalor, decay, rudeness – will be in for a pleasant surprise. Tokyo works. }

TOKYO WORKS BECAUSE people cooperate, and they cooperate because Tokyo works. Much has been made of the notion that Japanese society operates on consensus, yet it remains largely true. When you live and work in close quarters, respect for others becomes part of you. Japanese schoolchildren are taught collaboration, and as people grow older they build in elaborate self-censoring mechanisms. Inconveniencing others is just not done, and an outright insult is beyond the pale. In other societies this is called good manners, but here it's just the way things are. It's difficult to imagine Tokyo any other way.

THE MADNESS OF the crowds, the din, the bells and whistles, the waves of people who sweep you onto a train if you stand still, these fade away when you can walk into

17.

{ }

a neighbourhood shrine and be totally alone for a few moments. Should you drop your wallet, three strangers in the crowd will bend to pick it up for you. Should you step out onto the street looking the wrong way, you may be almost run over by an old man riding a bicycle at breakneck speed while puffing on a cigarette, but he will slow to miss you and watch over his shoulder to make sure you haven't got into further trouble.

TOKYO IS A CITY where little things matter greatly: a small kindness, a token gift, a friendly nod of the head, a temporary holding of the tongue. This is, after all, the land of the netsuke – a tiny sculpted toggle used to hold a pouch in the Edo period, when a kimono had no pockets – and the mon, a subtle family crest worn on the kimono. The netsuke for the new millennium might be the charms dangling from mobile phones, today's mon the strong graphics of a corporate logo – the packages may be small, but the emotions speak oceans.

THEN THERE'S Japan's legendary hospitality. If you look lost, a local may drop everything to walk you to your destination, and once there your welcome might be a deep bow. Homes may be small, but no effort is too great for a guest: cool, soothing towels on warm summer days, tea calibrated to the season, a precision-poured beer, dishes prepared beautifully and served just so.

AND A PROPER Japanese goodbye means that your hosts will escort you out and wait, bowing or waving, until you disappear from sight.

GIFT GIVING *

{ *GIFTS FOR THE NEW YEAR, GIFTS IN MIDSUMMER, HOUSE GIFTS, SOUVENIRS FROM A TRIP, GIFTS IN RETURN FOR A KINDNESS, END-OF-YEAR GIFTS to co-workers, bosses, relatives, teachers, friends. A melon packaged in satin and still on the stem can be a prize, but so can a keychain or a packet of sembei (rice crackers) if given from the heart. If you've inadvertently returned giftless from a journey, train station and airport gift shops stock scarves from Paris, macadamias from Hawaii and pickles from Kyoto. }

THE PRESENTATION IS as important as the gift itself, as a gift successfully given honours the recipient. A clerk might wrap even the humblest package as if it contained jewels; traditionally, gifts are carried in beautiful squares of fabric and presented with both hands. To open your gift in front of the giver would appear immodest.

20.

TEA AND CEREMONY *

{ *** TEA CEREMONY IS NOT REALLY ABOUT DRINKING TEA, IT'S ABOUT CAPTURING A MOMENT.** Sadō (the way of tea) combines a tradition of hospitality with the finest of Japanese arts and crafts: pottery, kimono, calligraphy, ikebana, food, traditional architecture and garden design all have a place. }

ORIGINALLY THE PASTIME of samurai and Zen priests of the 12th century, sadō was formalised by the 16th century under the patronage of the Ashikaga shōgun. The steps on the way of tea are codified, appealing to the samurai sense of discipline and offering an important diversion in times of peace.

THE TEA CEREMONY embodies the spirit of wabi-sabi, which fuses simplicity, nature and humility. The meditative and spiritual aspect of the ceremony is enhanced by seasonal ikebana and scroll paintings, the precise selection of ceramics and utensils, the sweets accompanying the tea, and the views of the adjoining garden. These unite to create an experience meant only for the here and now. Enjoy it while it lasts.

23.

OPEN FOR BUSINESS *

{ *AT PRECISELY 10 O'CLOCK – NOT ONE MOMENT SOONER OR LATER – THE DEPARTMENT STORE MANAGER REMOVES THE THICK SILK ROPE from the brass handles and opens the front door, and for the next minute and a half the entire staff focus exclusively on making you feel like royalty. Ground-floor clerks stand before their counters offering a deep bow and a heartfelt 'Irasshaimase' (Welcome) to all who pass by. By 10.01 and 31 seconds it's over, and the workday has officially begun. }

CONSUMER CULTURE IN Tokyo is definitive of the city itself. People shop as they work – long and hard. While much of what's bought is for the buyer, an equal amount is the gifts needed for the complex social and business relationships. Many department stores are owned by the companies that operate the train lines, hence the sprawling retail clusters around the busiest train stations.

25.

MANNER MODE*

{ *** TOKYO LIVES BY ITS TRAINS. SOME TWO MILLION PEOPLE PASS THROUGH SHINJUKU STATION ALONE EACH DAY.** At those numbers, people learn to ride with respect. No loud talking aboard these trains: that would disturb the passengers nearby who may look asleep but never miss their station. And no speaking on a mobile phone either: that's what text messaging is for. People make way for the very old and the very young (who already know to slip off their shoes before climbing onto a seat). }

NOT ONLY ARE passengers respectful of each other, the entire train system leads by example. Circles on platforms indicate precisely where the cars will stop, and a delay of even a minute will elicit an announcement of apology.

SINCE THE LOCALS spend a good part of their lives in train stations, a wide range of services are available, including a variety of food options like kiosks, stalls selling bentō (boxed lunches), stand-and-eat restaurants, and even sit-down places.

26.

A ROSE IS A ROSE *

{ *PERHAPS THERE IS NO ART MORE JAPANESE THAN IKEBANA. EACH FLOWER COULD STAND ON ITS OWN** as a perfect representation of nature, yet each flower in an arrangement becomes something more than it could ever be on its own. Unlike Western-style bouquets, ikebana emphasises the space between the flowers, allowing each stem, petal and pistil to have its day in the sun. It uses many styles to find a flow, to fix and bend stems or strengthen straight lines, or to suit the setting precisely. Flowers help the big city feel the seasons, whether it's the delightful concept of the winter flower, called 'grasses' in Western countries, or the ephemeral beauty of the cherry blossom.

IKEBANA'S LESSON FOR humanity is as profound as a Zen riddle: each of us has our own particular, unique beauty, but what good is it unless it's shared, and what good is sharing if you lose your own identity? }

29.

AN IDEAL WORLD *

{ *** PRECISION-PRUNED AND HAUNTING, THE BRISTLY PINES ENCIRCLING THE IMPERIAL PALACE ARE MOST VISITORS' FIRST GLIMPSE** of Japanese gardening. More than just pretty arrangements of flora, a Japanese garden is meant to represent an ideal world. }

IDEAL WORLDS DON'T just happen, as is obvious watching a gardener at work. Pine needles are plucked one by one. Moss and gravel must be swept clean of debris with delicate brooms of bamboo switches, so as not to disrupt what's below. Flowers are clumped just so, and the placement of a stone can change the entire meaning of a garden path. Some of the most beautiful, classic gardens date from the Edo period: Rikugien reproduces miniature scenes from famous poems, and Koishikawa Kōrakuen is laid out to represent famous Japanese and Chinese sceneries.

AS BUSY AS Tokyo is, it's always a pleasure to take a respite in one of these gardens and enjoy the fruits – or at least the flowers – of someone else's labours.

THE COLOURS OF TOKYO

can be seen in the spacious parks,
green in spring like Yoyogi Park,
with wide lawns, trees and ponds,
and spectacular in autumn, especially
the golden leaves of the ginko trees.
They're great viewing spots for
cherry blossom, all pink and white
in spring – a canopy for romance,
karaoke and the drinking of sake.
Many, like Hama Rikyu Park, the
former duck-hunting grounds
alongside Tokyo Bay, provide a
stark contrast to the silver-grey
of nearby skyscrapers.

MOTIVATED*

{ * **'GAMBATTE!' (GO FOR IT!) YOU'LL HEAR IT SHOUTED AT FOOTBALL AND BASE- BALL MATCHES** and in the background at the road races that seem to be broadcast every Sunday morning. But you'll also hear it said in corporate boardrooms and at the start of the work day; even small children may shout it to their dads as they leave for the office each morning. }

'GAMBATTE' IS MORE than mere encouragement; the gambatte spirit is central to the Japanese psyche. It really means to do your best – and then exceed it.

YOU NEED THAT spirit to flourish in a city as energetic as Tokyo. Watch the commuters as they surge through the streets like Monday morning salmon. Pass by an office window at 8.30 that night and you might spy the full staff still hunkered over their desks. You'll see the gambatte spirit in the never-ending training of craftspeople, in the concentration with which a chef grills yakitori or precision-drips sauce on a plate, in the balletic wave with which a subway platform conductor sends off the train, in the golfers hoisting clubs in net-enclosed driving ranges, in the students who attend after-school classes at a juku (cram school) in order to achieve admission to a prestigious university.

IF GAMBATTE IS the Yin, its Yang is gaman: enduring adversity in the name of a goal. Churchill spoke of paying any price and bearing any burden in wartime, but in Japan that's an everyday approach to life. If a project requires all hands, all hands will be there, from the receptionist to the vice president. There's no attitude of 'not my job' and no whining – at least not publicly – when everyone is working.

BUSINESSPEOPLE WORK HARD, but they also play hard. Night time might start with dinner with clients at an izakaya (pub) for a young manager, or a fancy ryotei (luxury Japanese restaurant) for the CEO where a meal might cost the same as a used car. This could be followed by karaoke or a visit to a shoebox-sized bar where a hostess keeps the whisky and the conversation flowing.

SOCIALISING IS only part of the point; these informal settings, lubricated by the appropriate beverage, enable hara-tsūshin (a heart-to-heart; literally 'belly communication'). Deals are made and relationships cemented. Should you miss the last train home, about ¥3300 buys you a sarcophagus-sized enclosure at a capsule hotel surrounded by stacks of others – although they're usually for men only. If the boss arrives at work in the same clothes as yesterday, it's a pretty good bet what he did last night.

THERE'S A THIRD element to this puzzle, and that's kaizen: constant improvement. The rare compliment from a boss might be followed by 'and I expect even better next time'. That may sound negative to the untrained ear, but what he (or increasingly she) is really saying is 'Gambatte!'

IN UNIFORM *

{ *** APRIL 1. THE FIRST DAY OF THE FISCAL YEAR, AND FOR NEW EMPLOYEES THE FIRST DAY OF A CAREER.** In a traditional Japanese company, employees don't join just for a job; they join for life. A new salaryman might mark the occasion by christening the lapel buttonhole of his new dark blue suit with the company's logo on a pin, and a woman might don her first uniform as an 'OL' (office lady). The styles of their clothing may change over the years, but these workers will probably wear some sort of uniform their entire careers. }

CORPORATE LOYALTY IS no longer what it was, and lifetime employment is no longer universally expected, but even if they leave the company, employees may keep tabs on each other for the rest of their lives, still meeting socially into old age.

THE APPRENTICE *

{ * **IF YOU WANT TO LEARN SOMETHING THE JAPANESE WAY, IT'S AT THE FEET OF YOUR ELDERS AND BETTERS.** Sons follow their fathers into the family trade – some merchants have been in the Tsukiji fish market for 20 generations; monks spend decades training to be priests; sumō wrestlers affiliate with a heya (stable); and the city's best French chefs train in France, bien sûr. Many kabuki actors are born to the art form and training begins in childhood – the leading families of modern kabuki go back generations. Actors join a prestigious yago (studio) and enjoy great social standing – their activities on and off the stage attract as much interest as those of popular film and TV stars. }

THE EARLY TRAINING might seem unrelated to greatness: sweeping, carrying, chopping. But through this process, a young practitioner learns his or her craft inside out. After a lifetime of relentless effort, a master among masters might earn the title of Living National Treasure.

41.

BUILDING
THE FUTURE *

{ *TOKYO ARCHITECTURE IS currently among the world's most exciting and influential, }
with the traditional preference for the simple, natural and harmonious now combined
with hi-tech materials and modern building techniques.

COVERING THE WORK of the city's astounding record of three Pritzker Prize-winning
architects is an education in itself. Tange Kenzō led the trend with his whale-shaped
National Gymnasium (1964), his skyscraping Tokyo Metropolitan Government Building
(1991), which recalls a European cathedral, and the lattice-framed Fuji Television
Network headquarters (1996), a giant orb that looms like the Death Star over Tokyo
Bay. The roof of Maki Fumihiko's Tokyo Metropolitan Gymnasium (1990) takes on the
form of a metal insect; Andō Tadao's creations include the sleek Omote-sandō Hills
complex (2006), whose six storeys amazingly look like three from the streetside.

THESE THREE MEN are just the tip of the iceberg, as a new generation of Tokyo
architects fashions a new world.

THE FANS*

{ *BASKETBALL PLAYERS SOMETIMES REFER TO THE 'SIXTH MAN', MEANING THAT INVISIBLE PLAYER in the form of the collective spirit of the fans. By that measure, you could say that the team at a baseball game at the Tokyo Dome is 55,000 strong, cheering, chanting and blaring instruments in rhythmic cadences. It's a bit of a change from earlier incarnations of the sport here: during World War II, baseball players were required to wear unnumbered khaki uniforms and salute each other on the field. }

THIS BENEFIT OF the 'sixth man' is not exclusive to sports either. Attend a kabuki performance and you'll notice that audience members shout out the actors' names at pivotal moments. It may have a staid reputation, but kabuki is interactive: it was the popular theatre of the townspeople, rather than one of the art forms of the higher social classes, such as nō. When kabuki companies perform overseas, they often miss the encouragement from their fans.

45.

TRADITIONAL*

{ *TOKYO MAY BE ONE OF THE WORLD'S MOST FORWARD-THINKING CITIES, }
BUT IT'S DEEPLY KEYED IN TO TRADITION. Tokyoites follow the seasons almost to
the point of obsession. The year begins with a hush disturbed only by Buddhist temple
bells chiming 108 times at the stroke of midnight. February brings plum blossoms; in
spring office mates take karaoke sets and sake to party on blue tarps beneath the
sakura (cherry trees). With June comes tsuyu, the rainy season, and the steamy days
of summer are punctuated by the aroma of incense coils. Autumn's russets and burnt
oranges festoon the city's parks – and plastic versions adorn its shopping streets –
while the return of oden (fish cake stew) to convenience stores coincides with the first
gusts of winter. Only at the New Year does the city once again return to the rare, sweet
quiet that began the whole cycle.

OTHER JAPANESE TRADITIONS derive from Japan's two main religions, Shintō and
Buddhism. Many Japanese do not adhere to just one religion. Instead, observance

{ } takes the form of life rites from different traditions. Your Tokyo friends might tell you that they are born Shintō and die Buddhist, and they might marry in a Christian ceremony for good measure, even if they never otherwise go to church.

SHINTŌ, JAPAN'S NATIVE religion, goes back to prehistory and holds that nature is filled with gods called kami. Shintō concerns itself with purity, so visits to Shintō shrines tend to commemorate new beginnings: the blessing of a new baby, or the start of a new life in a traditional Japanese wedding. You might even bring a new car for a blessing.

THE CENTRAL ACT of Buddhism, which arrived from India via Tibet, China and Korea, is to achieve enlightenment, to escape the cycle of reincarnation on earth and move on to Nirvana. Most Japanese funerals are held at Buddhist temples, and butsudan (Buddhist altars) to ancestors are common in Japanese homes and businesses.

TRADITIONAL THEATRE INCLUDES classical nō (a minimalist, hypnotic dance-drama) and kabuki. Both men and women acted in kabuki until the Tokugawa shōgunate forbade women on stage during the Edo period, a restriction that survives to the present day. Many male kabuki actors are, therefore, specialised in playing female roles.

TRADITIONAL PUPPET THEATRE developed at the same time as kabuki. It involves nearly two-thirds life-size puppets, manipulated by three black-robed puppeteers while a narrator tells the story.

THE JAPANESE CALENDAR is filled with occasions for joy or sheer exuberance; any festival is a great testament to that. Some traditional celebrations involve parading a mikoshi (ceremonial shrine) through the street and drinking a great deal of sake. Others are pure imports yet much loved, like the annual samba carnival.

THEATRICALS *

{ * **ALTHOUGH KABUKI ACTUALLY BEGAN IN KYOTO AROUND 1600, IT HAS NOW BECOME TOKYO'S SIGNATURE PERFORMING ART.** Its stories tell of bravery and suicide, samurai and courtesans, comedy and melodrama, and the costumes, dialogue, music and stagecraft can be unforgettable. }

AMONG THE SPECIAL features are on-stage musicians, assistants cloaked in black, and actors who break the action for ritualised poses called 'mie'. When an actor enters via the hanamichi, a raised walkway connecting the stage to the back of the theatre, you know it's going to be important. Many kabuki plays were originally written for the puppet theatre.

ALSO POPULAR ARE rakugo, a style of comic monologue that dates back to the Edo period where the performer sits on a square cushion with just a fan and hand towel; and manzai, highly fluid comic dialogue. Manzai draws large audiences to hear its snappy exchanges and clever witticisms about up-to-the-minute events in everyday life.

THE SOUNDS*

{ *JUST AS A VISIT TO ITALY MIGHT SEEM EMPTY WITHOUT OPERA, TOKYO WOULDN'T BE THE SAME** without traditional musical instruments. There's the twang of the three-stringed shamisen (like a banjo), mastery of which is an essential skill of a geisha. There are the hypnotic, stylised vocals that accompany shamisen, and the otherworldly tones of the shakuhachi (bamboo flute), which was played by Komusō warrior-monks in the 16th century. There's the ethereal, insistent chanting of Buddhist monks as they seek enlightenment, and the strumming of the koto (zither), as soothing as a stream on a balmy afternoon. Gagaku, which dates back to the ancient Japanese imperial court, is music performed by an ensemble who use both stringed and wind instruments. }

YOU MIGHT VISIT a theatre or concert hall to hear a performance or take in a festival. Otherwise, just listen closely at temples and shrines: you may hear music wafting, faint but ever-present, above the breeze.

53.

NOTHING QUITE STIRS the soul like the pounding, rhythmic roar of the taiko drum. 'Taiko' can refer to any of a number of large Japanese drums. Drummers who perform this athletic music sometimes play shirtless to show the rippled movements of their backs – adding a visual sensation to the auditory one. At festivals, drummers perform traditional or modernised dances which are choreographed to tell a story, keeping beat as they dance. Drum solos provide drama and as the rhythm speeds up, so does the intensity.

SHRINES AND TEMPLES *

{ *** A BUDDHIST TEMPLE CAN BE DISTINGUISHED FROM A SHINTÔ SHRINE BY THE DIFFERENCES IN THEIR ENTRANCES.** A shrine gate, or torii, usually has two bright vermilion upright pillars joined at the top by two cross-bars, the upper of which is slightly curved. A temple entrance usually has several pillars joined by a multitiered roof, and includes guardian figures. }

A SHINTÔ WEDDING procession through the courtyard of the Meiji Shrine takes place in refined solitude, very different to a matsuri (festival) in the bustling Buddhist precincts of Sensô-ji (Asakusa's Kannon Temple), yet both are signature Tokyo occasions.

THE MEIJI SHRINE and Asakusa really come to life during festivals. During Shichi-Go-San in November, girls aged three and seven and boys aged five dress in their finest (read: most adorable) kimono and appear for a blessing. At the Sanja Festival in May, some 1.5 million people crowd the streets of Asakusa to get a glimpse of the mikoshi, small portable shrines, being carried with vigour on the shoulders of loinclothed ensembles of men.

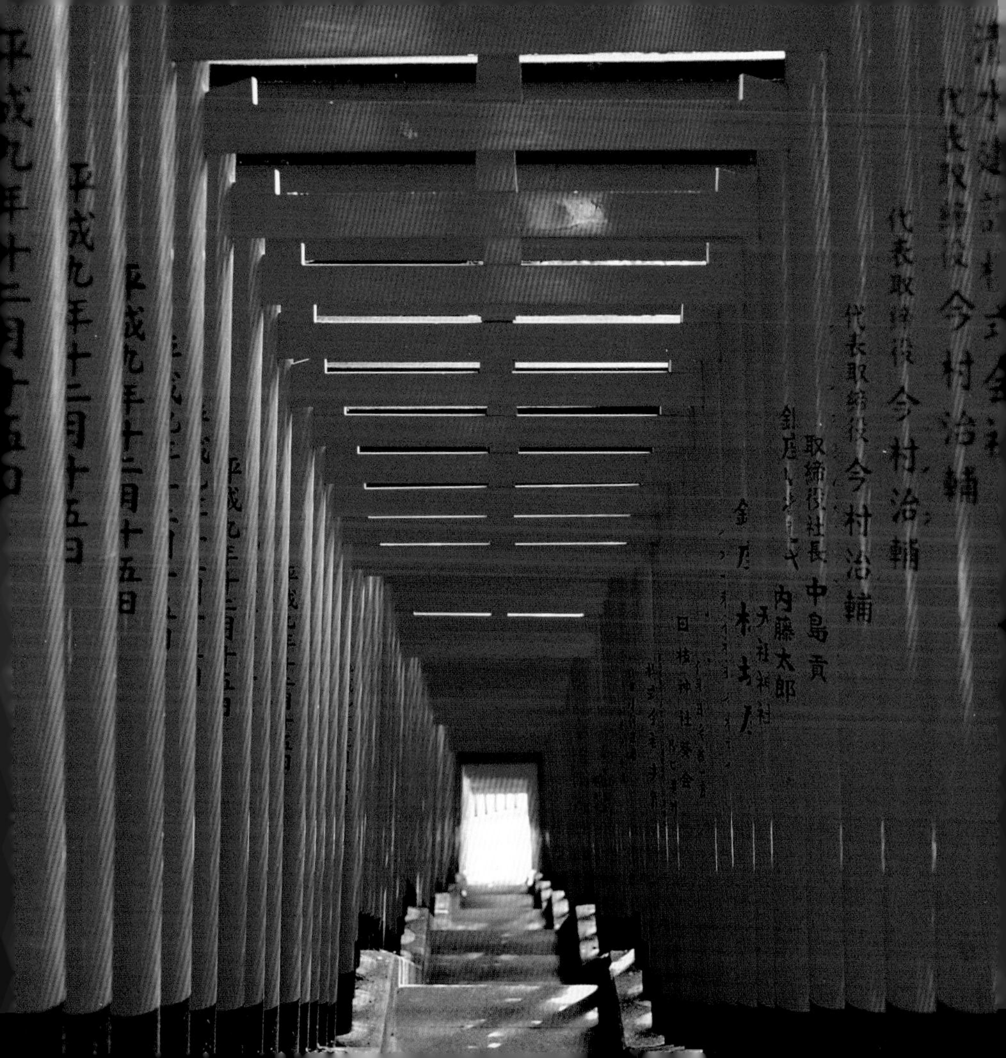

THE STREETS*

{ *WHEN YOU THINK OF A TOKYO STREETSCAPE, NEON, STEEL, GLASS OR GRAN- }
ITE MIGHT COME TO MIND, but stray a bit in the city and you'll find yourself in a
flashback to 100 years ago. You could be in the 'hide-and-seek' alleys of Kagurazaka,
lined with house restaurants offering rarefied cuisine and prices, where power brokers
broker power under cover of moonlight. The city's best preserved pre-war neighbourhood is Nippori, or catch the drums and chanting at prayer time at the Fudo-Myo
Temple in Fukagawa.

NOSTALGIA IS SO big now in Tokyo that even new indoor venues have got into the
act. Ō-edo Onsen Monogatari, for example, is a gigantic bathing house decorated like
a downtown of old. Yoyogi Park is a centre for cos-play zoku (costume-play tribe)
gatherings, which bring their own version of nostalgia to the streets by the Meiji Shrine:
young girls in Gothic make-up, blue lipstick or cartoon-nurse exaggerated outfits.

59.

BATHING BUSINESS*

{ *** A HALF-HOUR IN A SENTŌ (PUBLIC BATH) CAN TEACH ANYONE VISITING TOKYO MORE ABOUT THE CITY THAN ANY BOOK THEY'VE EVER READ.** Until recent decades, most private homes in Japan didn't have baths, so every evening people headed to a sentō to get clean. Company presidents rubbed naked shoulders with truck drivers and priests sat next to publicans. More than just a place to wash, the sentō was a kind of community meeting hall, where news and gossip were traded and social ties strengthened. }

AS PLUMBING MODERNISED, most of Tokyo's sentō went the way of all water, but some still exist. At Rokuryu Kosen the mineral-rich waters still bubble brown like cola, and Jakotsu-yu has a lovely rotenburo (outdoor bath).

SENTŌ ARE DIVIDED by gender, with both sides overseen by an obasan (auntie) who's seen it all so many times that nothing can surprise her.

61.

GOURMET *

{ * **A FEW DECADES AGO, WHO COULD HAVE IMAGINED THAT PEOPLE FROM PARIS OR PERTH OR PHILADELPHIA WOULD BE EATING SUSHI?** Or that wasabi would come to flavour mashed potatoes, that miso could be used to glaze codfish, or that we'd finish off a meal with green-tea ice cream? Japanese cuisine – healthy, delicious and handsomely presented – has helped transform the way the world eats. It's a wonder Tokyoites stay so trim!

GO OUT FOR DINNER – or lunch or even breakfast – in Tokyo and you're likely to see reminders of nature's seasons at every meal: matsutake mushrooms, oysters, chilled mugi-cha (barley tea), mandarin oranges, watermelon, chestnuts, sea bream, strawberries as big as a baby's fist.

JUST AS THE DISHES are works of edible art, the dining rooms they're eaten in can be exquisite sculptural spaces of wood, bamboo and tatami. Nearly every upscale place in town has invested in its interior design as well as its menu. }

IF IT'S NON-JAPANESE food you're after (though we can't imagine why), Tokyo chefs are often top class. A Japanese chef won the world pastry contest a few years back, validating what the locals already knew. From Thai to French, Indian to fusion, you won't need to search far.

EATING IN TOKYO can cost a fortune, but there's also the corner noodle shop, the little counter selling donburi (different items over a large bowl of rice), and that other staple, curry rice (a heaping bowl of rice on one side and curry sauce on the other). Vending machines on every corner, in every train station and every office dispense drinks both cold and hot. And you can always drop in to a convenience store for a bentō for your lunch, an onigiri (rice ball), a quick sandwich or a cheap and cheerful packaged ice cream. At the end of a work day, many wanting to avoid the rush hour stop at a yakitori or rāmen eatery, or a restaurant where the focus is on tranquility.

IT'S UNUSUAL to see someone eating alone: meals are social affairs and many dishes are ordered to be sampled by everyone at the table. The volume gets turned up a few decibels, and it is often a struggle at the end of the meal to see who gets the privilege of paying.

THIS BEING JAPAN, there are rules and processes to be followed when eating out. Diners are first offered a hot towel, a cup of tea and a menu. Before digging in, guests say 'Itadakimasu' (literally 'I receive'). 'Kampai!' is said when raising a glass for a toast, and everyone at the table checks to ensure their companions' glasses are topped up throughout the meal. And at the end of every meal, diners say 'Gochisō-sama deshita' (literally 'It was a feast').

HEAVY NOODLING *

{ *** RICE MAY BE THE STAPLE OF THE JAPANESE DIET, BUT NOTHING OCCUPIES THE JAPANESE PSYCHE LIKE NOODLES.** Tokyo is most closely associated with soba, the thin, brownish buckwheat affairs, but milky-white wheat-based udon, associated with Osaka, is equally popular. Both varieties are served in a large bowl of light, bonito-flavoured broth, or in warm weather arrive refreshingly chilled on a bamboo screen, topped with needle-thin strips of nori (seaweed), and a small cup of soy-based broth to dip the noodles in. Add wasabi and sliced spring onions for extra excitement. }

THEN THERE'S RÃMEN, about which Japan is – in a word – obsessed: a swarming bowl of Chinese-style noodles in broth, topped with something like sliced roast pork, bean sprouts and leeks. Rãmen restaurants are easily distinguished by their long counters lined with customers hunched over steaming bowls.

WHICHEVER NOODLE YOU choose, aficionados claim that slurping is de rigueur and brings out the full flavour.

KITCHEN TOWN*

{ *** SOME FOOD IN TOKYO DOESN'T EVEN HAVE TO BE EDIBLE TO BE APPETISING.** }
Restaurants throughout the city display life-like plastic models of every food imaginable, from a steak and chips to a bowl of rāmen, a plate of spaghetti bolognaise (complete with fork hovering above) or a pizza with only-in-Japan toppings like squid, corn and mayonnaise. Wash them all down – or not – with a foamy mug of plastic beer.

THESE PLASTIC FOOD models are sold at Kappabashi, also known as Kitchen Town, Japan's largest wholesale kitchenware and restaurant supply district. Here you'll also find colourful, patterned noren (split doorway curtains); pots and pans, some large enough to climb into; restaurant signs and furniture; innumerable varieties of tableware; industrial-size candy-making machines for the sweet tooth; and kitchen gadgets to make you go 'Hmmm?' – until you too find them indispensable.

68.

TSUKIJI FISH MARKET *

{ *** IF IT LIVES IN THE SEA, IT'S PROBABLY FOR SALE HERE.** There are acres and acres of fish and seafood – a world-beating 450 varieties – passing hands among wholesalers and resellers in an atmosphere of controlled chaos. Mountains of octopus tower near rows of giant frozen tuna, endless varieties of shellfish and tanks of live unnameables. It's not unheard of for a single tuna to fetch ¥20,000,000. Arrive before dawn to catch the auctions, but take care: the world's tiniest motorised lorries move pretty quickly among the market's often narrow lanes. }

LATER IN THE MORNING you can browse in the nearby outer market for the freshest of seafood and vegetables, or boots, baubles, baskets, plates and pottery. When you're done, break for a sushi breakfast or a cup of coffee.

SADLY, THE MARKET is destined to be dismantled and set up in new high-tech digs, computerised and more efficient. It won't be the same without Tsukiji's vast crowded canopy, the quietly boisterous hustle and the chain-smoking fishmongers in their rubber boots.

KAISEKI *

{ *THE ELEGANT, CEREMONIAL KAISEKI MEAL IS THE PINNACLE OF JAPANESE CUISINE.** In it, ingredients, preparation, setting and presentation come together to create a dining experience unlike any other. Born as an adjunct to the tea ceremony, kaiseki is a largely vegetarian affair (fish is often served, but meat never appears on the menu). It's a feast for the eyes as well as the palate, and like the tea ceremony it's best enjoyed in a private room overlooking a tranquil garden. }

THE MEAL IS served in several small courses served on plates and bowls carefully chosen to complement the food and season. Rice is eaten last (usually with an assortment of pickles) and the drink of choice is sake, followed by fresh-brewed tea.

UNTIL RECENTLY, KAISEKI was one of few options for vegetarians – an exquisitely expensive one. Today, however, many neighbourhoods boast vegetarian eateries, and some even serve vegan meals and exclusively organic produce.

74.

RADICAL*

{ *** TOKYO IS THE FIRST CAPITAL IN ASIA TO SEE THE LIGHT OF MORNING,** so }
perhaps it was fate that the future starts here.

ANY VISITOR HAS to be impressed by the futuristic cityscape. Shinkansen (bullet trains) whiz by at 280 kilometres an hour. Parking garages spin cars like Ferris wheels. Ferris wheels are as tall as office towers. Taxi doors open and close magically by themselves. Toilets have built-in bidets and seat-warmers. Elevator lights gradually brighten as passengers ride from a dark lobby to a brightly lit floor.

WHAT'S NEWEST, most advanced and just plain coolest to the rest of the world is just the way things are done in Tokyo. All you need to do is open the newspaper, filled every week with announcements of new inventions that just maybe will become part of our lives before long.

THIS IS, AFTER all, the capital of the nation that gave the world the Walkman, the fax machine, high-definition TV and the tiny mobile phone. The electronics of the future

{ } are on sale today in the shops of Akihabara Electric Town. Elsewhere, ferret out futuristic textiles or tiny masterpieces in the fashionable boutiques, check out the Design Festa Gallery and (in March) the Anime Fair, or just muse on the music of tomorrow at a club or music store.

IN TOKYO'S TRENDY Omote-sandō district the big names of fashion vie for attention. You'll find the next look along with lacquerware, wood-block prints and ceramics from both yesterday and tomorrow.

AND IF YOU NEED an ultracool gourmet product, browse with the OLs (office ladies) and obaasan (grannies) in the cavernous food halls in department store basements. Black truffle oil or dark chocolate truffles? Sushi vinegar or dessert vinegar? Pickles, pickles or pickles? Or any of hundreds of grades of the new season's green tea? It's all the food of the future.

TIME WAS WHEN almost every stall in the hall would offer samples, and the savvy snacker could make a sheepish lunch out of it. Though that's no longer the case, you can still try sublime chocolates, sesame-seed sembei rice crackers or gorgeous, flower-shaped okashi (sweets).

SOME PEOPLE THINK that the impulse to innovate may come from some sort of competitive spirit between Japan and the rest of the world. Others believe it's unique to this city, that Tokyo's congenitally hard-wired to keep just slightly ahead of the curve. Either way, we can't wait to see what's next.

NEON*

{ *** STEP OUT OF SHIBUYA STATION AFTER DARK, AND YOU'RE IN THE TOKYO OF YOUR DREAMS.** Giant screens and pulsating towers of neon encircle Hachikō Plaza, streets radiate out like a starblast, and those with diligently acquired elegance mix with trendy teens in go-go-go get-ups. }

A FEW STATIONS north, the perma-glow canyons of Shinjuku provide less innocent fun, though they're no less of a draw. Tiny bars are stacked one on top of the other in stiletto-thin buildings. Kabuki-cho, Tokyo's bawdiest district, boasts massage parlours, love hotels, pink cabarets and strip shows, all well attended by drunken salarymen. Female voices wail out invitations, while punks eke out a living passing out ads.

ONCE TOKYO'S SO-CALLED floating world was an ephemeral place of night pleasures, where kabuki actors, prostitutes, poets and high-living merchants cavorted. There's little left today in the way of sentimentality; the night pleasures mainly involve a sleazy underworld of illegal Southeast Asian sex workers, controlled by thoroughly unromantic yakuza bosses.

80.

{ *** THE TERM 'ANIME', A JAPANESE WORD DERIVED FROM THE ENGLISH WORD 'ANIMATION',** is used worldwide to refer to Japan's highly sophisticated animated films, just as the term manga refers to Japanese comics. }

THE WIDE-EYED WORLD of anime exploded into the West in the late 1980s in the form of the apocalyptic visions of *Akira*, and graphic arts worldwide have not been the same since. Japanese animation alternates herky-jerky motion with lush photorealism, iconic storytelling with characters not of this world. If you'd love to have *Totoro* as your neighbour, you are ruled by *Princess Mononoke*, or you've ever been *Spirited Away*, you've got plenty of company in Tokyo. By some estimates, 5000 anime titles are produced annually, and manga comic books account for 37% of all publications sold.

UNLIKE ITS COUNTERPARTS in other countries, anime targets all age and social groups and covers all genres. The manga and anime aesthetic colours everything from advertising graphics to street signs and fashion.

TOKYO TECHNO *

{ *** THE SHINKANSEN (BULLET TRAIN) CAN TAKE YOU TO THE FARTHEST CORNERS OF JAPAN,** but you needn't go that far to see the future. In Ôdaiba, Miraikan (the National Museum of Emerging Science and Innovation) mixes high-tech environmentalism, a planetarium inside an orb and robots that do just about anything. Toyota may be an earthbound company, but its Mega Web showroom is firmly of the space age. }

STEP OUT TO LOOK back across the bay and see how far you've come. At night, the skyline becomes a rainbow-coloured electronic tapestry. The erector-set Tokyo Tower, which epitomised the future when built in 1958, now looks quaint and almost cute.

DESIGN IS BIG in Tokyo, and each April and November its Design Festa brings 45,000 people to see both experimental and populist designs in areas such as video, furniture and fashion. The National Robot Exhibition holds a biped walking robot competition some years, and each November attracts engineers and robotics experts alike to check out the manufacturing gizmos as well as less industrial gadgets.

PRADA TO PUNK *

{ * **THE WIDE BOULEVARD OMOTE-SANDŌ IS OFTEN REFERRED TO AS TOKYO'S CHAMPS-ÉLYSÉES.** That may be overblown, but the two streets have one thing in common: they're at the leading edge of world fashion. From the chic lines of Prada and Dior to the elegant scarves of Hanae Mori and the ripped-and-reconstructed look of Comme des Garçons, this street and the alleys around it host the haut-est of haute couture and ready-to-wear. }

STEPS AWAY, YOU'LL find the cos-play (costume-play) kids by Harajuku Station. Tragic and powerful, the Goth-Lolitas primp and pose for the cameras, finding self-expression in their transformative identities. And on the cacophonous side street Takeshita-dōri, the world's most fashion-forward teenagers snack on chichi crepes as they hunt for clothes and accessories that won't catch on elsewhere for another two years. By which time, of course, they'll be on to the next newest thing.

90.

GOLD STAR

TOKYO WINS A GOLD STAR FOR
ITS ATTITUDE OF GRATITUDE. THERE ARE
SEEMINGLY ENDLESS WAYS TO EXPRESS
APPRECIATION: WHETHER FOR VISITING,
WAITING, FOR A JOB WELL DONE OR
FOR LOOKING AFTER SOMEONE. THERE'S
EVEN A PAST TENSE OF 'THANK YOU' IN
JAPANESE. BEHIND THIS SENTIMENT
IS THE BELIEF THAT WE ALL SOMEHOW
RELY ON EACH OTHER, AND WHEN
WE ALL THINK THAT WAY, WE'RE RIGHT.

MY PERFECT DAY

ANDREW BENDER

{ * Jet lag will probably provide the wake-up call you need to reach Tsukiji fish market before the sun rises. Rubber-booted stall owners and an army of hydraulic lifts work toward selling a fish every four seconds. Then break for the breakfast of champions: the freshest sushi in the world. Hop on the subway to Asakusa, once the bustling centre of shitamachi and still the spiritual heart of Edo, where Sensō-ji is Tokyo's grandest and most-frequented Buddhist temple. In the afternoon, take a peek into the future in the electronics and manga mecca of Akihabara or steep yourself in tradition with the fabulously made-up and costumed stories of the deeds of the samurai at the kabuki theatre; the legendary department stores of Ginza are right nearby. As night falls, try to tear yourself away from the avenues of neon to commune with the fashionable teens and tweeners in Shibuya, or rise above it all with dinner in Roppongi Hills and a 360-degree night-time view amid artworks at the Mori Art Museum and its observatory.

}

YET ANOTHER LONELY PLANET AUTHOR WITH AN MBA, ANDY HAS BEEN SHUTTLING BETWEEN THE US AND JAPAN SINCE THE 1980s, working with Japanese companies in finance and entertainment and later as a writer for publications including *Forbes*, *Travel + Leisure* and the *Los Angeles Times*. He maintains his business chops with cross-cultural consulting. Find out more at www.andrewbender.com.

PHOTO CREDITS

CITIESCAPE

TOKYO

OCTOBER 2006

PUBLISHED BY LONELY PLANET
PUBLICATIONS PTY LTD
ABN 36 005 607 983
90 Maribyrnong St, Footscray,
Victoria 3011, Australia
www.lonelyplanet.com

Printed through Colorcraft Ltd, Hong Kong.
Printed in China.

PHOTOGRAPHS
Many of the images in this book are available
for licensing from Lonely Planet Images.
www.lonelyplanetimages.com

ISBN 1 74104 938 5

© Lonely Planet 2006
© photographers as indicated 2006

LONELY PLANET OFFICES
AUSTRALIA Locked Bag 1, Footscray, Victoria 3011
Telephone 03 8379 8000 Fax 03 8379 8111
Email talk2us@lonelyplanet.com.au

USA 150 Linden St, Oakland, CA 94607
Telephone 510 893 8555 TOLL FREE 800 275 8555
Fax 510 893 8572 Email info@lonelyplanet.com

UK 72-82 Rosebery Ave, London EC1R 4RW
Telephone 020 7841 9000 Fax 020 7841 9001
Email go@lonelyplanet.co.uk

Publisher ROZ HOPKINS
Commissioning Editor ELLIE COBB
Editors JOCELYN HAREWOOD, VANESSA BATTERSBY
Design MARK ADAMS
Layout Designer INDRA KILFOYLE
Image Researcher PEPI BLUCK
Pre-press Production GERARD WALKER
Project Managers ANNELIES MERTENS, ADAM MCCROW
Publishing Planning Manager JO VRACA
Print Production Manager GRAHAM IMESON